AF512732

From the dunes of life

From the dunes of life

Kaushik Banerjee

ADROIT

Adroit Publishers

NEW DELHI • KATHMANDU

ISBN 978-81-87393-20-7

2020

Copyright © Author

All right reserved.

No part of this publication may be reproduced or transmitted
in any form or by any means, electronic or mechanical, including
photocopying, recording or any information storage and retrieval system,
without permission in writing from the publisher.

For sale in the Indian subcontinent only.

Published by
ADROIT PUBLISHERS
4675/21, Ganpati Bhawan, Ansari Road, Daryaganj, New Delhi-110 002
www.adroitpublishers.com

Typeset in Garamond Premier Pro by Arun Sharma
Akriti Graphic Solution, New Delhi-110 081

Cover Design by Rupambika Khandai

Contents

Foreword

Kaushik & I are from the same industry. We first met about two years ago, when I joined my current organization. He is a colleague and a dear friend. We hit it off pretty well, our chemistry is less to do with our work and more to do with our tastes and inklings in life, be it being attached to anything related to solitude of nature and its divine beauty, our diehard passion for the hills and obviously my interest in his poetic talents.

I have read most of his poetry and can conclude that there is much more depth to him than what meets the eye. It is said that poetry is a law unto itself, and that there no standards whereby it can be judged however of the 'sonnet' style of poetry, it is not entirely true. A sonnet consists of fourteen decasyllabic lines, rhymed according to prescription. Kaushik's poetic talent has the undercurrents of 'Shakespearean Sonnet' and hence the reference here. His poetry talks of 'life herein' and what could be 'life beyond life', the fragile wrongs we have done in life, the ambitions and passions we all have and some we bury to follow societal norms, the frowning on the herd life we all live, the frailty of human behavior et al.

I wish my dear friend a very satisfying and successful life and congratulate him on pursuing his dream of writing. Your poems and words resonate with my thoughts, they unshackle something deep and meaningful inside me and I am sure it would, for many of your other readers.

I wish that one day, when we are both free from our worldly duties and mundane lifestyles, we will have our tryst in the mountains somewhere, in the cold of winters, where we will discuss literature, poetry, our families, deeds done well, life well lived and the years gone by. One day I am sure, we will.

To quote from one of his poems "Hope is life, there is nothing else, and the dunes of time, is our lives"

Cheers to that, cheers to life!

Aman Thakur

1

The tree of thoughts

They keep trimming the plants of my garden,
My mind is fertile, I am a bunch of thoughts,
I feel the pain of cutting and sorting,
The one can't defend, shall live in rots!

They say it will grow again, I meekly agree,
To the process of curtailed living and space...
They keep changing my positions for ever!
They keep me away from decaying disgrace!

It's a withering process of plastic growth,
I am a tree and shall always sprout,
Away from fear and adorable weaknesses,
Life is lucid and I have no doubt...

The problems of this society are large,
They only ruin every living being...

ooo

2

Your anger

I know you are angry, I am sorry not guilty,
Although this feeling is very rare...
It does not matter to the rest of my mind,
Some corners I am thinking threadbare...

While situations shall remain indifferent,
Nothing shall change at these ages...
I reckon stupidity of myself and yours,
Trust me they will pass like pages...

Of disengaged time, thoughts and people!
Of your chagrins, and of my outburst...
On the death bed, who cares who knows?
What memories, pulls one down first?

The ship shall sink, both yours and mine,
The wretched, the monks, shall ride same boat!

ooo

3

The stars reflect

On the heights of greatest mountains,
A feeling of hill top and the stars...
The stars are kind of further steps
Assuring! Better place remains far...

The mortal has limit, but not emotions,
Wish of everlasting equanimity for all,
The unfathomable, the yet unknown,
I am so hungry, I am still so small...

Altitude one must travel, and respect,
Creates differentia, builds anomaly,
Of the basics that are just fooled by self,
Of things that are acceptable respectably,

I wish we could touch the stars...
Why live always under limitations?

OOO

4

Near Death

What to do with unwanted favours,
When pain sings dreams to eternity,
When the end is whispering so close,
No more feelings no more anxiety...

A stage where wishes, prayers and mind,
Are congruent only for freedom,
From the agony and the continuity of it,
A moment of no ecstasy or boredom,

Where blood, tears and sweat feel same,
The penultimate of the ultimate,
Where nothing is superfluous, nothing sane,
No one is wrong and nothing is legitimate!

On the death bed and hours before,
Is another story which has no trash...

OOO

5

Another insight

Nothing can be changed on this world,
The air the water, nature of a being,
Things could only be contaminated,
Or there is a different way of seeing...

The metal, the warmth all get mixed up,
The feelings, sobbing's, giggles and more,
Substances, matter, and all that matters,
On earth that we can count and score!

Way above the head, deep under the feet,
The growing the rotting of everything,
Breeding and brooding of blood and flesh,
The pristine clarity of existence in nothing...

Going "by the nature" is just a myth,
In polluting one that God has created!

OOO

6

Joy of giving

Joy of small things, bliss of giving,
Someone parts the other a smile...
These are moments of compassion,
When emotions flow and grow agile!

A morsel for one can be big for other,
This realisation comes with giving,
It is not reciprocity, neither gift,
For few good souls it's a way of living,

What gets exchanged remains on earth,
There are nothing that eternity takes...
All we hide, cherish and don't part with,
Are our ignorance and our mistakes!

I promise to do whatever bit I can,
Not expecting them to come back...

OOO

7

Trivial

Unreached app food, and waiting spouses,
Someone scolded my child in school...
Why they drive like this? Reasonless honking?
Why all service providers, are nothing but fool!

This dress could have been better,
Else's perfume! Superiority, inferiority...
Nasty demeanour, worried for future,
Which makes us loose the priority!

He, she, doesn't love or understand,
They, them, shall never comprehend...
There is no peace, even in pieces,
Normal living shall live, will transcend!

In-front of ocean, at the cremation ground,
It's again just like, lost and found...

OOO

8

To pass on

Why hard learnt truths are just passed on...
Why to kids and the meek only?
Why these dreams, failures get communicated?
Without judgement, almost completely!

The stair's too wide for all,
Everyone, everything shall become...
Something or other in this abstract,
Flawless are none, Great are some!

Live for the life you were born to,
Whatever it takes, whenever it gives,
Whoever owns the responsibility shall...
Keep gauging the time, when one forgives,

Something's should not be passed on,
Let's digest them in our bowels...

OOO

9

Contractions

Agnostics, prejudiced, insane and prodigal,
The visibly, intellectually, different group!
The rich, the poor, the dark and the fair,
Topologists and primitives, all in a soup....

In the process to learn the basics,
So much learnt, and yet ignorance!
Ages, gold, and expensive patience!
What all not spent? For arrogance...

A protest, against the incomplete?
Inconsummate, the weak and incapable,
The tussle between science and occult,
The best God and the most stable?

How fragile, and vulnerable thoughts,
To live one must die many deaths...

OOO

10

Ablaze

Although I am silent, I am ablaze...
And it's not a matter of being in greys!
Identities, or be it otherwise...
The insider has stories, the liar says!

This quiet is so similar, so familiar,
Many speak and one listens!
No loud mouth or hard perseveres...
Same preaching's, same lessons!

You are one, or there are many?
That unhinges my symphony,
So much toil, distances covered,
I still believe, I have been funny...

In my ways of living, within myself!
I look up, to know you better...

OOO

11

Character

Someone presume of someone's state,
Before sanctity, it is too late...
Presumption are based on ideas of self,
Assumptions remain privy to regret,

God's never came down, times made think,
In moments we have just another wink...
The isolated ones, the not so alone!
What will not survive will surely sink,

Bold eyes can watch through things,
Audacity is not only about wars...
Attitude does not ask always to win,
At times good time, also scores!

Sanguinity is a trait, not character,
What needs culture, needs devotion...

OOO

12

Listening and talking

Listening to too many opinions, is trash,
Times change, be it good or bad...
Real life is never bombarding problems,
Thoughts and opinions make it sad!

The minds reveal our scare and love,
Love is beautiful, scare is repulsive...
Respect turn into affection eventually,
Hate makes people impulsive!

Every mind has character, if not open,
To woes, silos, or public wrath...
Some choose to remain unpolluted,
A larger lot, takes a different path!

Spending time in understanding others,
Is worse than smoothening own ideas!

OOO

13

Pattern

I don't have any pattern, I am alone,
In soliloquy for ever, skin and bone,
Predicaments, overwhelmed predictions,
Love is my only addiction!

Mankind and the freedom of all,
When shall we stop eating dead?
Animals or the losers forever...
Wrong is wrong, is what I have read,

As a child I lived among species,
Nothing wrong in their reclamation,
Let all have space, respect space!
Trash I say is religion and nation...

May that wink, and that face...
That power is not only for me!

OOO

14

Fetching

The sweet little inspiration, at one corner...
Off the world, I have an unpleasant frown!
Love for that simple smile and thought,
Fettered myself, in this social lockdown,

Pulling myself back to me again...
I realise there's a world to take care off!
Family, neighbours, society and country,
News ways to think, shall cut-off!

Yet that blink of ecstasy, the beloved,
Who has never uttered a word...
That another being I beseech to know,
Albeit I have not seen, and never heard,

Repose in your beauty my dreams,
Shall fetch you, that's purpose of my being...

OOO

15

Remain quite

I will not call you, don't want to mess!
I am afraid and in deep degrees...
There will be another morning,
Sure to see... just another place!

Remain in your hearth, I will survive,
I wished to know, your kith and kin,
The one look, which is overrated!
Only stance! Is not what I have been!

Times to come shall bestow fruits,
I am not nuts...I have remained exacting,
For millions of years along with loss,
I am not striving, I am not fighting...

You remain calm, I will not utter a note,
Let's see, how far things rule the roost

ooo

16

Perils

Today we are threatened, of many things,
Death is the only reason I see for mankind,
Friends and family losing each other!
Which is inevitable... aren't we blind?

The movement of things be good or worse,
Creates excitement, it's the speed always...
The doctors and apples, won't be alive!
No one cares, is what nobody says...

Menace, perils and expectations!
Time keeps rolling, there's nothing else,
Man proposes, God disposes,
Every other thought, is just nonsense!

Listen to this calm, it's so very filling,
Open your eyes, there's light still around!

OOO

17

Don't discuss

"I wish no one had seen me"
Is a jargon that can keep us agile!
Who said no-one has done wrong?
Why your wrong is so fragile?

Mistaken, we remain with silence,
Loud mouths are ones who hide!
The followers are common people,
They stack up on the heavier side...

Our behaviour is very situational,
Our demeanour has many claws,
World runs faster towards death,
Ignoring its own merits and flaws!

If there is something amiss...
World is in a mess, don't discuss!

OOO

18

Bigger for

Doomsday may come or may not...
So many things remain worrisome,
People and dreams and then the both,
And endless desire to just become!

The way one thought as a child or adult,
Poor people, rich ones, and their wishes,
Survival from pain, the sweet success,
What not is endangered, from our dishes?

Culmination is another thought, they end,
Everything on this mud, water and air,
Termination is eventuality for mortals,
Let's think sane, let's sail fair...

Eternal strife is a far bigger foe,
Wish to be safe, healthy and wealthy!

OOO

19

The lost one

He wanted to regret on a tiffin box story,
He believed, those days epitomised glory,
One wrong jargon, one fault forever...
He remained benign...he is still sorry!

And thence-forth roads kept running,
Merciless movement of finding peace,
That child who was behind nothing,
None stopped him, nature or disease!

Yet reminiscence of the younger one,
Are buried and carried to far off places,
In soft slumber, life remain alive,
Juxtapositioning events and faces...

He is neither alien, nor a friend,
He shall remain as another being

OOO

20

Predictive

When the worst can become worse,
Situation off-course is adverse...
Thoughts fail imagination there,
The holistic shapes up as a curse!

Predictability is the reason of worry,
The unforeseen cause's distress,
This is the predicament of successful,
When arrogant stammers, what a mess...

State of mind is certainly, consequences,
Confidence is measured from visibility,
Matter of time or mysteries of faith,
Decide every individual's agility...

Hope is life, there is nothing else,
And the dunes of time, is our lives...

OOO

21

The good news

The Good news is! There is no bad news,
We must sail and we must cruise...
This world would never disintegrate,
The way we live, is the way we choose!

Our thoughts are overwhelmed by media,
And media is another excuse...
While we fame, defame people or places
Stupid influence, is again abuse!

The whole mankind is flame of lanterns,
Controlled by few, manipulated by blues,
Individuals can never stack up to none,
Generations will always snooze...

Good news is that we are under God!
He or She shall take us further...

ooo

22

Spine

One must own or disown completely,
The underlying hatred or favour,
Things don't stack up, they never do...
It's all about anticipation, and flavour!

Likes, dislikes, love, and prejudice,
Early mortality is a different jargon,
One sees and does, what is but prudence,
Systems disagree, yet someone is on...

In mending, smoothening, caressing, alive!
End is a decision, people jointly agree...
Wherever, whatever are the disagreements,
What matters is, only the degree...

One who can't stand up and own,
Is the one, who never had a spine...

OOO

23

Questions

Living within either or, neither nor...
If people don't appreciate, it's failure!
Unsure direction is complete loss,
Age and adages, walk along akimbo,

The knob of lantern, leaders, rules the roost,
The unsuccessful have nothing to boost,
Prayers and wishes remain unheard,
At one point of time one should...

Change the course and pick up new,
Before one is ready for adieu!
One can ask all questions they wish to,
Others can't answer, everything...

Syndrome of one, allies with empathy,
From others...but to what extent?

OOO

24

Hoping and hopping

The lanes and by lanes of every city,
The hearth of the poor and the sad,
Where sunlight and fresh air is seldom,
Yet rain keeps pouring, winter is bad...

Employment threatened, is life threatened,
Not for the ones who still have a choice,
The unfortunates, the harsh reality ones,
People who don't speak, yet listen to noise...

When things are worse, every corner has it,
No reason, no blessings, nothing restores...
Intellect abandons naturally with wisdom,
There remains no love, the world abhors...

That's when a speck of hope shines!
That's when people value hope...

ooo

25

Another night

There was a day, my father said...
Think of your potato and bread!
I am poor, my Dad was poor,
Yet I learnt somethings for sure!

Learning, beseeching, amidst all odds,
Among proud, honest, people and frauds!
I smile my own texture for nothing,
Get smiles and frowns, as well as nods,

Times change, change is welcome,
The weakest is now stronger,
Smiling back to the best challenges,
Everything, has just grown longer!

The plat of the platter and more,
The walk of insane, and obvious pain!

.ooo

26

Dark retreats

There is nothing called "end of the world",
One more chance is always welcome...
One more toll, another barricade,
Looks challenging maybe to some!

Realign, revamp, and resurrect yourself,
Opportunities are lying at every corner,
It's a matter of picking the cherries,
And was never about him or her...

Dreams of hope...and hope to dream,
Wishing to sleep, wanting to stand...
When shaping up is a far sighted view,
Toiling hard under the sun and sand!

To begin with, is the only new thing;
Culminating is but eventuality...

OOO

27

Unenclosed

From bosom of love, yet another glance,
Terrains of stories and territories of chance,
Without you life, is always superfluous...
Sumptuous feeling of complete dance!

What shall one do? If you keep failing?
Without directions, stars keep falling...
It was never you, but this feeling alone,
Amateurish depths, their endless calling!

So very incomplete, with far off success!
Minds and ideas, make and break...
A rare smile among blossoming youth,
A moment where nothing is fake!

They are as costly as our feelings,
We don't understand, either of them...

OOO

28

Paths and the walk

Change is not an event, it's a walk, to walk,
Everybody drives something or the other,
Idiosyncrasies and conviction and fancies...
The outcome, shall be visible together!

Journeys are adventure, as well as painful,
When journey is the end, why not begin?
While it is well known and also visible,
Yet this frown on the face? What a sin!

A sweet beckon from the heart of hope,
And distant hills, become meaningful,

People around...their million thoughts,
Wishing to see lives or things in shape,
A greedy, persistent, inborn pursuit,
Of not letting go, and neither escape!

ooo

29

Coarse

You beseech and I want to reach,
Corners are different, unfortunate,
Genesis of issues, remains unheard,
Then finally some says its fate...

Why shouldn't I demand my rule?
Whatever it be, however miniscule?
This wish of culmination, rejuvenation,
People can't be forever in school...

I will bury myself under obligations,
Don't need anyone to resurrect me,
I stand tall within, forever, as I am,
It never reflects on my physiognomy!

Let world take its own desired course,
Let things ferry the way they want to...

OOO

30

The skin

The skin reflects life within...
Till a particular age, everything is skin,
Life moves and always keep moving,
We are worried when can we begin?
The new of anything upon the earth,
Survives in between foes and kin!

Expectations don't back all dialogues,
Some remain unfettered like the time,
Array of thoughts, for and against!
The simplest livings does rhyme...

An old friend, who can come along,
Play the same tune, sing the song...

An eye that looks at the surface shall,
Remain worried for ever and ever!

OOO

31

See and listen

Unfortunately words are not visible,
Or else life could have been legible,
Both reading and hearing are reflexions,
Feelings would not have been inevitable,

Jumping from well to well of voices,
Listening to words and their choices....
If one can see, there is no need to hear,
This perpetual open space for noises,

Eyes don't often but phonetics meet,
Mono syllables have erotic greet...
They shape up to love or violence,
Apart from lies this earth was so sweet!

At last this amateurish greed to perceive...
Whatever they tell you, you know the truth!

OOO

32

Face to face

You seem familiar, I must have seen...
In may be a book, or fiction on screen,
It was no different but the cold eyes!
And the "what not" pursuit, I had been,

You were neither the beauty, nor the brain,
Yet I came back to you, again and again...
Habits are powerful, they shape our wishes,
The "used to" attitude, and the refrain!

Better, tastier, is something accepted,
Unknown, wishes will be neglected!
The more years we know ourselves...
The less, lesser, and least is reflected!

On my own I presume and assume,
Doesn't matter to you, was so well known...

OOO

33

Another break

I left you to take a long break and felt,
Many things were hurting under my belt,
When I returned from this perfect trip,
I had lost my rhythm as well as my mind,

Without you everything was easy, boring,
With weary eyes, I kept on exploring...
There was some loss which kept pulling,
Some truths and lies which I am living,

Without you music was far far better,
I was with nature without a fetter...
I love you, Mountains, Sand and Brine,
Thinking of them I am feeling fine!

Alas things do culminate, always...
I am back to mundane, and my work!

OOO

34

Radicals

Love is standalone, with lust it's consummate,
While they might look like the happiest mate...
Oh love! I was after you, for so long...
The well unknowns, remain that great!

Being busy imagining, which one is better?
Life is too short and years are very few...
Deep roots when naked, never look familiar,
Shake the self-up, before they say adieu!

Isn't it, the matter of all matters, is peace?
Once peace is achieved we go for fun...
In pieces both remain exacting!
On this earth, under this Sun...

If a smile beckons the body and soul,
It's probably worth smiling back...

OOO

35

The birth

Greed, lust or alcohol, Is the father of all...
Poor man is thinking, how to save the child?
I am drunk and I don't care!
Short stories can equally be wild...

Still caught up between leg to, or go late,
Equanimity I loved, has changed to hate!
At times I still think, of leaving it to fate...
Bother for any? If I am not, no one is great,

There is a population, having sex for fear!
Of non-performance, betrayal or money,
I want to shrug this feeling from my shoulder,
One that looks true, is not so honey....

One melts down to stand up again,
Molten within, yet uptight! Mother earth....

OOO

36

Seldom freedom

Being generally sad, is never captivating,
One must cry or shout, in top of his voice,
Anthropy was so much beloved...
Philanthropy never became a choice!

They who live, singing their songs,
The happier lot, the better fortune...
Nobody wanted to die as a beggar,
We all array to live, without a tune!

Love and respect, are two best known,
Verdicts have longer laundry list,
The ask is too big, one falls ajar...
Among cautions, amidst twist!

Let them be one against us all,
What's wrong in fighting for freedom..

OOO

37

Every last breath

When I call, it's worthless... avoidable,
When people speak I must socialize??
A hermit crab shall so remain...
In these notions of paradise!

To smile one must bent few sinews,
For people around, its a greater task,
Pulling legs made us happy for years...
Happiness is in the act! Don't ask,

If something made you laugh for long,
They aren't alone, you are forlorned...
Fighting within and carrying the spirit,
What a love, that stays honed???

To make a point, to prove again,
My every last breath, will be alive....

OOO

38

Understanding

Now I understand, what you meant!
My mind earlier had a separate bent,
In understanding one, is happiness!
In vain, again, this life was spent...

I can still hear songs of playfulness,
Me and myself playing around the truth,
Now it's so warry, so absolute insane,
Realising the potholes, and broken tooth,

I don't know one day, it won't matter...
Days to come will have longer stories,
One that believes, shall have many lives,
Others will fall in quirky categories!

Alas having understood you repeatedly,
I understand, I don't wish to understand!

OOO

39

Best failures

I have done my best...I can't do better!
I am sorry, I hate you, break the fetter!
Real life is me and my kind of people,
I am sorry to say, I can't be greater...

From good days to bad, and history apart,
The song of a story, and stories of songs?
I am broken and I don't wish to care...
Happiness is somewhere the thing belongs!

Despair, prejudice, the persistent pessimist,
One happy soul must go down this list?
It's my way or one may not array!
If not ecstasy, a smile, amongst, amidst...

When there will be space, I won't disgrace!
This petty world for asking more...

OOO

40

Another thought

Anything that's covered, shall burn or rot!
Eventually everything will be non-existent,
Where is the choice between ego or love?
When time and space are the only constant,

The points of a point, remains unidentified,
Losses of the lost, will stay agile...
There are footnotes for everything known,
I still beckon... The age old smile!

They all continue to live happy or sad,
My worries, will persist in me,
It is always a matter of fate and time,
That shall, reflect in my physiognomy,

That place is which place? I got covered?
When the end is same, we will meet again!

OOO

41

Alibi again

There is a new pack...if you are capable,
Nothing but this journey...if you are able..
Rearrange, resurrect, it's the only motion,
All convictions can never be stable!

Enough love is inconsumate, stale...
Expectations, reciprocation, very male!
A last word, another story...
Shall keep us, in shades of pale,

Jumping to different, hopelessly,
Is not the right attribute,
Thoughts and people, are always ajar,
None has the beckon, neither flute...

One must say! To be heard,
One must react, to act...

OOO

42

Prey to all

When the lips are zipped, it's again amiss,
Nobody trusts nobody, that's truth of life,
The game of power, and it's manoeuvre,
The contrast of a job and wife...

Victory and shame are equivocal,
God has blessed us, not to be in war,
Silent complaints, recurring pain,
Many reasons to just abhor...

It won't be us, cannot be either,
Nature shall play, fate shall play!
Nothing is sustainable, none almighty,
It's just time and we all are prey...

Let's culminate...That's the beginning,
Deep vision and hard thoughts...

OOO

43

Maintain vanity

The common, takes gruel some shapes,
Respite is dream, just peace escapes...
A leave from mundane, another rejoice!
The lively mountains and to landscapes,

The break out is difficult, sanity, insanity...
Amateurish effort to maintain vanity,
People just act and people behave,
Where on this earth is humanity?

They say you counter this and that!
We all wear a different hat...
While individuality is a matter of else,
Lives get hammered to be in format.

Alas this is a blessing in disguise,
Or else men shall turn to animals...

OOO

44

The Shy

I never spoke, you did not say...
Food and work, always in array,
The easiest way to kill a shy,
Is just to shy away...

The hands of greed, always need,
To consume more and breed...
Similar thoughts of more and more,
Higher hunger, higher the sore!

Complex within, shade all colours,
Sleepy minds have dreams asleep...
Compulsions and regularity of it,
Make everything, normal and cheap,

There is another shy I know exists,
In my home and across everywhere...

ooo

45

Acquaintance

I want to forgive, and forget as well...
People don't allow that room!
I am cleaning and trying my best,
Can't live for ever with this broom...

Cleaning own house, is duty forever,
Where noses never gets raised...
Basic duty, minimal requirements,
Old and new have never embraced!

Moment of surprise, house stands broken,
Value is never envisaged by us...
In between, amongst rules falling apart,
Everything else is nothing but fuss!

Can still absolve, may again acquit,
A morsel of love, keeps me alive...

OOO

46

The balance

I was talking, but I did not expressed,
Matters get endorsed, and suppressed,
Poor me and the likes of me...
Survive denial for everything guessed!

You coming back, is another miracle,
I shall strive to die my own death...
A handful of dreams, a bag of expectations,
One must survive for own breath!

The way challenges are getting stronger,
Times, decades, eras and more!
This permanent feeling of lost control,
Of sizeable, visible, and the roar...

Can't forgive each other but then,
It's only a dream for equanimity....

OOO

47

Planning

Planning can take you places, if you survive!
Planned will be executed, thought is naive!
"Man proposes, God dispossess"
Failures, surprises, threadbare arrive...

Surface is expectations, bottom is lies,
What all and what won't ever arise?
Measures are too old, development is new,
It is neither the weight, was never the size...

Hands on we were, plans were sighted,
The vision of time, at the time of visions...
The super confident, the utterly confused,
Every individual had their own reasons!

"When the going gets tough, the thought gets..."
Another bunch of sighs and regrets!

OOO

48

Sages of time

Today is, yesterday was, tomorrow will...
Yet this solitary existence of a will!
We stay softer...we remain hard,
Burning in our own mess, our grill,

To hold or to run away is choice,
Choices are often biased, there's more...
Wish to be free, the want of achievement,
In dreams one keeps, this self-adore!

Time is money, money is land...
Land is nothing but higher access,
To opportunities, beyond mundane!
Ramakrishna, the sage, defined success...

Let now be the time, it shall rhyme...
Sages can't define what is yours!

OOO

49

The persistent

Waiting for doomsday or retirement!
Kids to fulfil dreams, is another craving,
The common man, the poor housewife,
Everybody is just behaving...

Some leave again, few do come back,
Such weak and dry, the sun can burn...
Whose reaction? What remedy?
Get punished, whenever we act stern!

To hold, behold, are different airs!
Impending, obnoxious, the cruel, alive...
Impatient world, indifferent God,
The hermits return to their bee hive,

Never ending delay and restlessness,
Is the treasure, we all measure...

OOO

50

The walk

The perpetual feeling of guilt was built,
Over years of negligence and slumber,
Mistakes kept piling up and then it all fell,
Finally in a stage where numbers outnumber...

All deeds were owned these decades,
So many and so much was done...
Happiness within, and future in eyes,
The walk, the distance, so much fun!

Finding reason to be lost again...
Loosing was never a negative word,
Because it was different in some way,
Memories are always absurd...

Game of life, and its changing rules,
Is where feelings sleep and dream...

OOO

51

Doesn't work

Four fifteen minutes, make an hour!
Unfortunately life doesn't stack up...
Plans, dreams, moments of crying within,
Wrinkles, mistakes, reality and close-up!

Often wonder...to correct or repent?
Minds are so very difficult...
Isn't the winds that decided?
We are all preys... nothing is cult!

When the face was sweetest...
Other things mattered more!
Childhood in all ages do galore,
Reason why elders won't abhor!

Whom to pity, forgive, or forget?
Homogeneity is so contagious...

OOO

52

Morsel

A morsel from your pretty being,
Took me to the umpteenth cloud,
Swag is something that was unknown,
I had never been so loud!

Some moments for whatever reasons,
Shall have a recall which is ageless...
Unexpected favours, galore of memories,
Beautiful people, make us aimless!

It's aura of words, or the demeanour,
It's all real, however fake...
Or the hunger when everything is wow!
Feelings compel us, to commit mistake!

It was just a favour I know...
Albeit my expectations were something else!

ooo

53

Closed

Competition within! Family and friends,
Ugly situations, and growing trends...
Simple living is so complicated,
Everything bends! Good things ends!

A moment of respite, then hours confused,
Just a thought that keeps engaged,
The seldom pop up of nasty feelings,
Growth in peace, remains ungauged!

If I can't move out of myself to talk,
To listen, to think, to do and to not...
I will never be born to see this world,
I will die within my own thought...

God's keep my eyes open,
I keep my mind closed....

OOO

54

Embrace

You embraced! And touched my heart...
It was so lonely otherwise,
One nice face, last good feeling!
Birth is nothing, amidst lies...

The unexpected, was a wish,
Mundane never ever surprise...
Far off or maybe deep within,
Always believed we are wise!

Feelings galore...years move on,
What was important was the size,
Lower, higher, deeper, and vanity,
Expectations die when person dies!

Motley with one body and soul,
Faces, people just arise...

OOO

55

Unlikely

Being ashamed is not only blasphemy,
Being alone is equal sorrow...
Thought you understand, but understandings!
Are things we often self-borrow!

Deepest beliefs are in soliloquy,
But heartened bliss is around people!
In this search, within beseeching,
One must bend, eventually steeple...

The old Gods are but helpless...
So much change and so fast?
The radical mind and conscious heart,
Beings don't turn up, things don't last!

Prodigy brings smiles, and upbringing,
Genetically every morsel is unlike.,

OOO

56

Sudden attack

One fair smile, one wrong look...
Everything goes out of the book!
Genesis of thoughts, food for soul,
Cook and eat! Or eat then cook?

Ugly jealousy, or handicapped zeal?
Out of the box and beyond the learnt!
What to do? What not is better?
Equivocal ideas of the heart burnt...

Normal creates chaos, or its opposite?
Son and father, and father and son...
Ages gone, civilizations drained!
Long dried under this scorching sun!

Incorrect, inconsumate, thoughts alone,
Drive us to our own destinies...

OOO

57

Difficulties

Why prepare for fight? There are better things!
To do and not to do...it's a phase, will evolve!
Tough days, difficulties, is only providence,
Things will bake in, world shall revolve...

A person and his cornered thoughts,
Jeopardy to self, without askance...
Two a tango, more a threat!
Imaginations, possibilities a chance,

Let there be light, it shall come with time,
Someone too bright, can fade away...
It's unpredictable, it's shame and pain,
Everything necessarily can't end in dismay!

Let the thoughts take its own route,
It's a river that will keep flowing....

ooo

58

Let's roll back

Everyone wants a life without rules...
Self-convictions are good enough?
Society, animals and human...
The jungle remains too rough!

Good, bad, ugly are owned yardsticks,
It's individual! Community can't save,
Mistakes of life, misses of being...
Before almighty one pretends to behave!

Restoring things and relationships,
Is the worst and most difficult part?
Misdeeds of ignorance and times...
May give another opportunity to start!

My friends when eyes open, its morning,
Sooner the better, change is change...

OOO

59

Only you can

You looking at me, and I watching you,
God! Both of us are so helpless...
One thought here and another prayer,
I am so weak, you are so less!

This waiting to culminate or begin,
Is at times so unpredictable...
We keep watching each other then,
This moments so weak, you so able!

While everything is controlled by you,
Why am I so inconsumate?
Aware of fallacies, am aware of faults,
I need a corner, just love me or hate!

My talking to the inexistent is shame,
Truth is that I still believe...

ooo

60

Nothing more

This hush...and the rush,
People right and things wrong...
Unmelodious, inexplicable truth,
What relations? Whose throng?

One must defy oneself to push!
Everything is another ambush..
Lords will never come to rescue,
From one corner to another bush!

Things are defined by them, for them...
Why on earth do we act berserk?
The rest of the all, is the real problem,
There shall be someone to be quirk!

Wake up to see the truth, anticipated....
It's all expectations, it's nothing more!

ooo

61

Too old

Too old for these threats and ecstasy,
One must go slow and easy...
Changes often and realisations new,
Activities less! Thoughts keep me busy,

Cohorts attract, similarities beckon,
Virtue or vice, one fails to reckon...
This permanent, pertinent ask for better,
Is something I sigh to remain unknown!

Many folds of verity, know, forgotten,
Stressed for every, weak limbs and weary...
Procrastinations and misbeliefs!
Times spent, time lost like dreary,

Blessings blossoms on equanimity,
Dreams come live! Once accepted...

OOO

62

Hauled

Looking back at your eyes, to memorize...
The solace that loves me, in trying to find,
A voice that whispers music aloud,
Half a soul! I remain confined...

Cryptic thoughts, in the deepest seas,
Wishes written on clouds, yet covered,
A little more of you in my space...
Yearnings that cannot be discovered,

A covet so brimming with desires,
That familiar askance in your gaze...
They keep me holding, to my breath,
I sniff in sighs and remain amaze...

Ship that sails and never gets wet,
In being around you, I am so far...

OOO

63

Canvas

This vast canvas and another lonely night,
Me and my colours, ink, and thoughts,
Soliloquy, mundane, and my own self,
Worries, plans, predicaments and lots,

Good old friends and family astray,
Seemingly wanton, feelings array,
Lost and found within myself!
Hope and vigour shall see new day...

Amongst this amiss, deep in the storm,
If one has to shout, the other is too far,
Or else they don't understand you...
Neither is it a wishful bazaar!

Looking straight into my eyes,
My soul is still so alone...

OOO

64

With you again

I will walk down the memory lanes,
With a friend, what I wanted to show!
Happiness all around all over...
Wish list of decades, anything else is No!

We shall walk woods and swim again,
And talk without thinking,
The soul will see some lights now,
These eyes will stop blinking!

Another moment, another rain,
Confidence, shame, shall remain away,
That love again...that stupidity,
Hunger is taste, realising anyway...

Don't blame me, if you can't make it,
Winds are whistling some old songs...

OOO

65

This feeling

This pertinent feeling of loss,
Ages gone in earning wages...
The incomplete, the incapable,
Living in corners, living in stages!

That wish to see you and talk,
Those feelings, deep down the drain,
In wishes, lives a soul forever!
A sunny day, and another rain...

They become us, I become no-one,
From one dream to another idea...
Thoughts of better green and sleep,
Longings for nothing but panacea!

Tarot, numerology, what soothsayer?
It's all in us, where we deserve to be...

OOO

66

Point

Pushing works till the edge, not beyond...
People just keep rubbing, they are fond,
Of putting else into misery and laughing,
The balance, the pity...the vagabond!

Fall start after the pinnacle, isn't it?
Where it breaks, and cannot be stretched,
Family, colleagues, friends and more...
There are situation that can't be sketched!

"What if?" Becomes another repose...
Thinking, blinking, without direction!
Lost as to what travelled through,
This feeling of guilt, without correction,

Beyond a point, there is no point...
Is something gathered from hearsay!

ooo

67

Generations

Son you behave different now,
I know you are growing up!
These infidels, blossoms, this you...
I am worried, you are showing up,

You can shout at me, because I did!
Age and maturity is my conviction,
You are right, you shall remain...
My truth! My worry is my valediction,

Son you should give it back!
To the wrong, to the inexplicable,
Against your wish, for your good,
I shall remain stable...

Son we have been consumed by thoughts,
Now that's what people call generation gap...

ooo

68

Calling you pal

Pal we used to stand together,
Now there is no strength in our feet,
Time changes, its further changing!
To regain aplomb, when can we meet?

Friend you made me feel holistic,
I am hopeless and helpless without!
You, whom I dumped for race of life,
Left nothing in my mind, but doubt!

I have forgotten, favours done, received,
I am in spiritual pain like you...
Broken limbs and broken heart!
I wish to start that friendship anew...

Alas I can't move through predicaments,
And you can't hear my voice, anymore...

OOO

69

One more breath

Time of a breath from you,
One look and I shall remain hence...
Your overall impact, my clumsiness,
Rest is all fine but difference!

This wish to have a tete-a-tete,
And lost prayers of mine...
Will go with me with end of time,,
I shall keep saying, "I am fine",

One more smile please! On this earth,
One more moment to be agile!
Just you and me... couple of minutes,
Another existence, another smile...

Lost in me, my cravings and empathy,
Still trying to figure out, who are you...

OOO

70

Hearsay

People say and people hear,
The listeners are who live in fear...
Of losing even the mundane!
Or looping in something dear,

The wider they listen in numbers,
The greater is the might of leader,
These gaps in between all of us,
Some accept, some turn pleaders,

Modern lanterns can be controlled,
Every individual has a knob...
To keep inspiring or pursue wrong,
Is yet another destined job!

People will never stop their pursuit,
Acceptances are but dispute...

OOO

71

New beginning

Tomorrow is the only space,
To forget bad taste and disgrace,
Why this lagged feeling for new?
For all commons! It's only a race...

Facing next day is but obvious,
One can't culminate over night!
If past was full of insecurity,
The bright sunshine will remain right...

Let's keep running for ourselves,
Idle folks never have a say...
The earlier bird catches her prey,
And slower ones shall face dismay,

Tomorrow is life, hope and belief,
Yesterday shall always be drowned in grief...

ooo

72

Noise and light

The light is too bright, things are not right,
Another feeling.... nothing to write!
Too helpless in ego! Weakness and sight,
Feeble can never describe might...

The noise is too loud, yet I am aloud,
Competition between incomparables...
Nothing unlearnt, across ages!
Thoughts survive in monosyllables,

She comes back and takes me over,
The daily, doesn't allow me to thrive...
At times I am a happy person again,
They pull my lapel to another drive!

There are too many distractions to see,
Very few may be I shall live through...

OOO

73

The loss

I am bete noir to none, I just want to live,
I wish to fall in love, my wish is to give...
Seldom this heart reaches out!
To jargons of wish...to forgive...

Some eyes that never follows a recall,
Are the ones, I am defined for...
Something or maybe someone's glare,
Yet this perpetual, everlasting abhor!

Last when I had anything sweet...
Was ages ago, even before my birth,
Moments, days and years lost in search,
I can still smell and fantasy that mirth!

Come lost eyes, faces, to my demise,
I am still in the lookout for new...

OOO

74

From within again

My this stubbornness, and me are closet,
Nothing can touch us when we are together,
Sane, insane, human or feelings...
There is no-one, who can change the weather,

We are so lonely and yet so complete,
We never care of victory or defeat!
No eyes, no ears neither any senses,
This is complacence, when we meet...

So much lost for this lust and love,
Between us both are always above,
Each other, and teaching beseeching...
It's all bloodshed and no one's a dove!

Among us we are poised to see death,
Peace and mercy are too worldly...

OOO

75

Incomplete

Need a new life to fall in love again,
Your eyes are too far for me to see,
Albeit this feeling of keeping away,
Disengaged! This feeling to disagree!

There is nothing bad in falling in love,
Life is all about the feet on earth...
Hatred and this contagious naggings,
Makes one forget, death and birth,

My God and yours, both are indifferent,
We all are in the platform of rent,
Whatever suits, whoever looks good,
Who cares of beauty, neither accent!

Holistic peace, remain inexplicable,
Is another wish of the incomplete...

ooo

76

Eyes of God

There are a pair of eyes...
To start with and to end well,
These thoughts beseech repose,
This heart needs to dwell!

Forgetful I remain in me,
Shying away from myself,
Another shrug, disengagement...
Going further down in deeper delve!

That look of giving away things,
The sweetness of nothing but a smile...
Of broken promises, of real life,
The reason of your being fragile!

Alive in feelings, deep in you...
This life has found a solace!

OOO

77

Serendipity

There is no happiness but in serendipity,
These people and parties are stupidity,
The yard stick is own, and life disowned,
Expectations are nothing but rigidity!

Yes the wish for God, luck and dreams,
Without miracles and catastrophe!
Some corner of mind, completely blind,
Rest all are fools surviving on hope...

"A day shall come" is another wish,
"Things will change", "You will see..."
What all and what not in sacrifice,
Uneven reasons, to disagree!

Change is the only visible truth,
Everything thing else is verity...

OOO

78

The boat

The deeper, the darker, this deliriousness...
Where fading away is just like breathing,
Only rhyming friends, without evidence,
Fallacy and rituals, are another thing!

It was a pond which borrowed my heart
Without emotions I strife for fullness...
This refrain forever and the forgotten life,
Is another malady and another illness!

One who changes, is always in motion,
The cold, tasteless is someone's choice,
And chosen are the very few...
What ado about this smell and noise?

Somewhere deep within, some insights,
It sails alive as a forloned boat...

OOO

79

Lock Ness

The soul at loch and serenity...
Reminding me of the living dead,
The cold weather and warm Scott!
I am left without a heart and head,

Which God painted my love "Ness"?
Back at my home I live in disgress,
You remain sublime in single malt,
World's eternal strife, is world's distress!

I shall or may be my body again,
Back to the woods, castles and sane,
Another glimpse of the mesmerising!
No word unsaid yet all in refrain...

Countries wide, habitats different,
Will never allow this elopement!

OOO

80

To be heard

A wish to speak out, with no one to listen,
Is time spent in thoughts and digestion,
A moment of victory and complete defeat,
A stage of answers without the question...

Pondering is something, we necessarily do,
It's a phenomena without much ado...
Accepted one's, and the common folks,
Not every colour is adorable as blue!

Recollections was never a negative word?
Where we speak of heard, unheard?
What's so complete, with other living?
Discussing the first, second and third?

Sounding is superior than to discern,
The more you wish, the farther it is...

○○○

81

Mind-frames

Love is measurable and limited,
Where peace supersedes all justice...
Be it home, community or nation,
Limited mind-frames are all practice!

One can run again! All are born free,
Every moment and landscapes...
While still young, won't eat, defeat!
Alive in ends and holy escapes...

Smooth surfaces shall not reveal,
Fire alive in a sleeping zeal...
Content consciousness in the winds,
Awaits a lifetime of fair deal!

Lawful, illegal and legislature,
Can never ever create peace...

OOO

82

Wish to be alone

She had a name, I have forgotten,
Without control life sails...
In predictive apologies, I am myself,
In isolation and its trails!

She can't be found anymore,
Heart of thoughts, and food for soul,
I beseeched for that one position,
Someone or something just stole...

Away from me, distant for ever,
She had her own adorable living,
There was nothing but realizations,
What pity in dungeons and then giving!

She was someone I knew for ever,
She is my wish to be alone...

OOO

83

Glorified

That friend never had a name...
I am all in tears and shame!
Follow, unfollow is all social,
Played well, still lost the game!

He or she, was aspiration to be alive,
Lost link, of people who can drive,
Plenty is still so far away from us,
And meek faces, looking to survive...

Let all see our God's and prudence,
Thought process and repeated nonsense,
Views can be different, it's all crazy...
What matters is only the lens!

Stupefied, glorified, another way to live,
Renewal of attitude is the only truth...

OOO

84

Hard days

If you start early, you may have your fill,
Shorter time left is another thrill...
Select priorities as they come and go,
Pondering in between will fetch you nil!

Many truth, realities, digested over time,
The wish remains for peace and plenty,
Running after the "shorter the route..."
Something that begins from age of twenty!

All numbers are for achievements only,
Be it tranquillity, or any other final goal,
Time rolls on and gives no time,
In doldrums, unattended, this soul!

No one knows, can neither anticipate,
This perpetual mock drill called life...

ooo

85

Fathomable

Little happy, is kind of unhappiness,
None is content with half food or dress!
These measures are bad, they make us sad,
The real problem is, no one can address...

Insignificant toil, is like no work done,
Just to prove the self, and realign,
It's a moment as inconsumate, as lie!
This world has its own design...

Running behind, shall never be the truth,
Every limited thing, creates desire...
Love, money, satisfaction, or peace,
Incomplete will always be on fire!

Cents or kopeks individuals have counted,
Fathomable wishes are but expectations...

OOO

86

The compromised

Eventually growth is all about age,
Everything certainly changes to grey,
All that are cryptic possessions!
Shall remain in only, hear-say...

Family, friends and remaining lot,
The wish the want for felicity...
Desire to move away from this maze,
Dream to touch the infinity!

There's nothing called prudence or luck,
It's the contempt or the admiration,
These years are only for experience...
The culmination of solitary dictation!

To compromise over and over again,
Can make one a rebel! Ask for freedom!

OOO

87

Fuming progress

A day of calm, without alarm...
A night of slumber, with peace!
Another moment my wish to change,
Again a minute, to hold on and cease,

The thunder, the anger, the love within,
The very wish to challenge everything,
I am not happy, I am not equivocal,
Joy of actualisation, completion of sin,

Every individual can think enough...
Thoughts never can have limitations,
To survive the feelings, and remain alive,
The distance allure of material imitations,

Sleep is in solitary, not fuming progress,
A craving want, is renamed a wish...

OOO

88

Forest

Haste-full days and sleepless nights,
Weary eyes and looking at expectations,
Work or home it's all in mess...
Expectations from relations!

No room for mercy, no space to care,
Neither time to think threadbare...
Expecting the unexpected always,
Nothing pairs is another despair!

Year after year the procrastination,
Belief, trust, everything lost in vain...
The basic nature, the heart and soul,
Looking for every trash again!

That used to make sense sometime!
Alive in the deepest, thoughts of forest...

OOO

89

Left over

There is still so much left in the bowl,
The privy of fortune and public foul...
So much love and care ignored!
Days spent as crows, and nights as owl,

Sweet faces, feelings and relationships
Better known for ends than beginnings!
To digest the very inconsumable,
The fruits apparent before twinnings...

Yet so much to see and bliss unfolded,
Smaller pieces, the bigger the smile!
If routine changes from desire to truth,
Every ignorance has its own style...

Expectations, love, consequent condolences,
There is so much stray, wasted for none...

ooo

90

Galore

This wish to see starry nights, cool breeze,
This want to move from concrete to home,
A traveller at heart and also a family man,
Nothing is complete, wherever I roam...

No more dungeons, the forgotten hooky!
Time, money and identity crunches...
My sweet little kids, and my predicaments,
Pride and melancholy all coming in bunches,

Many expectations shall see my demise,
Fighting for breath, water and more...
Things will remain...in juxtaposition,
The array of thoughts, and feelings galore!

Not too far, yet away from dream...
Small acceptances, and short life!

OOO

91

Disguised

I thought your family was absolute sync,
Yet member's never said what they think,
The clock moves on, it's quite and fast,
Some remain in thirst, some still drink...

When glory was ablaze, you were God!
Consummate epitomised you for long,
Alas the pain the normal have seen,
The poor yet never became strong!

I don't know whether to laugh or cry...
Destiny astir and eventuality supreme,
I never thought I could ever be close,
Neither in aspire nor in dream!

May you sleep well, my verity is turmoil,
Forgive me if I have smiled in disguise...

OOO

92

Facts and fiction

God is misfortune and fortune is God,
Something's are great others are old gate,
The topsy-turvy, the hullabaloo...
Are neither prodigy nor fate!

If one may wish to see through the things,
Soothsayers, palmists what all rings...
This dilemma is complete in itself,
Happiness, sorrows along it brings,

Every want for change, demands rearrange,
All stupid endeavour, is another dream,
Of different and yet the difficult most,
However lucid and benign it seem...

Then everyone is a traveller at heart,
All facts and fiction remain astray!

OOO

93

Sigh

Either you have not spoken for long,
Or no one has patiently listened you ever,
It is the silence the meat of endurance,
Which is too hard, fast and clever...

The quite is always not meant for peace,
There are many who keep breeding disease,
One open arm, one single effort,
A little while to smile and cease...

Opportunities or maybe the helm of them,
However small and dis-agreeable...
The new, the bright, can't always be right,
An endless wish to change the "stable"!

God has given this prolonged sigh,
They have meanings one can't deny...

OOO

94

Dismay

I should have fallen in love, twenty years back,
With someone like you, whom people admire,
Time is gone, now what apart from cryptic?
Left over in dismay, I'm nothing but desire,

It isn't repentance, it isn't just another wish,
It's a matter of deep thoughts in anguish,
A soft hand caressing a wound...
The want to come over, the will to vanquish,

You were agile, within million smiles,
You were kind and will remain amorous,
Truth with time, and eyes with dreams,
When time competes with most rigorous,

There is nothing young in feelings or mind,
Unforgettable shall keep haunting us all...

OOO

95

Still afloat

Two old fools can still find solace,
Too old schools and natural grace!
Acquaintances without known relation,
Where to hide under which face?

The unknown desire, the flame, the fire,
The mellow respect in sumptuous admire,
Of the close and the yet too far...
Off the inconsumate and entire!

What remains silent and is still loud,
The hidden secret of the proud...
Amateurish want for the best of world,
A wish for rains with the darkest cloud,

Too many thoughts to delve deeper,
Why not just remain afloat?

OOO

96

A new member

The responsible, the inseparable, the father!
Of an about to, a new born or a grown up...
The amorous heart, the blinking eyes,
The wish to become a mother with makeup!

Love flows without reasons or belief,
The platonic, the crazy and the saint,
It cannot be confined under prejudice,
It is a different stroke, it's another paint,

Some affinities can never be defined,
Like some truths which cannot be explained,
Every one suffers for acknowledgements,
Affection is natural, why are we drained?

Welcome to whoever can lend a smile,
Welcome to protest just being alive...

OOO

97

Hello

Seriously! Where were you?
Could not find a charging point,
And what is it you look like?
I am nothing more than a man,

Do you remember anything, anyone?
I guess I had fallen asleep...
So what all do you recollect?
Believe to have survived death,

Had life been hard, or your people?
Wish to experience something new,
Have you got money or anything?
Only thoughts, without memory,

What is your journey from here now?
Shall walk down unknown paths...

OOO

98

To my son

Your chagrin is different, my problems are alive,
I'm unhappy like you, yet we have to survive,
We all don't know what to believe...
Where to gauge and where to dive!

Son! This trust is a matter of time,
You engage or disengage off and on,
That is where we learn and keep learning,
Whatever is here shall all be gone...

All I wish is that we remain positive,
Look forward for better days...
There shall not be darkness forever,
A bright smile with new sunrays!

Son it's a matter of time...
When you shall be me and I shall be you!

OOO

99

Affinity

A sweet smile and an amorous face,
With due respect to the dignity...
Poor people, old people!
Young and rich, crave for affinity,

Either this feeling flows or grows,
From one being to another or within,
Most efforts apart from basic needs,
Is for love among all thick and thin!

To rise in self and make the changes,
From turmoil's to the heart of lakes,
Complete sympathy, to total bliss!
Trues friends, to incompetents and fakes.

Few more lines of the ever wanderer,
In the search of simple love...

OOO

100

Tomorrow morning

Tomorrow will be better, I want it that way,
Some old goodies, some new arrivals!
Many demons in mind, and complexes,
Living in commotion, living with rivals,

Lost control! Which is the basic nature,
Of all beings, inspite of the wish to rule!
We know the sun shall rise with warmth,
New thought process to make us fool...

This new is hope against all learnings,
However common and mundane...
Preaches us to remain salient!
What all and what not in this brain...

One smile may God bestow on us,
To lighten up just this tomorrow...

OOO

101

Walking for self

I shall again walk alone in eyes,
To think things inside out,
Wish to punish myself together,
Without questions, without doubt!

When prejudice has been ruling,
Unwanted songs of various notions,
Trapped in self-contained thoughts,
Fettered in stupid emotions...

I shall speak to myself for days,
To understand my understanding,
Seamlessly to discover truth!
What's wrong and what's according...

Of faces, places, situations and more,
That make me walk yet another mile...

OOO

102

Treasured aplomb

Colours on my eyes and money in mind,
Everything travels without my knowledge,
I am in control of my wallet and more...
I am trained to survive on the edge!

What not I have? What not have I lost?
I shall gasp forever...yet epitomise aplomb,
There is nowhere, discussions can take,
The dead shall remain in their tomb!

Equanimity comes with age and wealth,
Poverty and health are another song...
The doldrums of mastery, and confidence,
The belief on self, where nothing is wrong!

Let the world sail through, I shall pray,
From predicaments to the wishful peace...

ooo

103

Corners

I disown my wish! The parody and English,
This craving for new rules and peace...
Stray between penultimate and ultimate,
The joy of survival in every disease!

One who lives, knows the tricks,
Connecting the abstracts, time is gone!
A little tweak here or there is fate,
And culminate to a reason unborn...

Unplanned is horror to its own demise,
Yet man proposes, God disposes...
Amidst consummate and Inconsummate,
What seems like open abruptly closes!

When everything is harpooned to one life,
They never get back to wishful corners...

OOO

104

A meek child

Trends of own dismay, own wrongs,
And people who go with the throngs,
Predicaments are self created!
There is nothing but sad songs...

The second life, once I recover myself,
Is so untrue? And against the lot!
In my contradiction, ages contradict...
In my vision, everyone forgot!

A frail smile of a weak child, yet owned!
Ownership is not only about task...
A benign thought, a feeling of calm,
The melody of unforgettable mask!

Some moments survived! Some clear vision,
Is all we long for, to see at the end...

OOO

105

Guided

One fine thought, one resolved belief,
One single change advised by all,
One last thing, that can never revive,
One small thing that is not so small,

The idea, prudence, in one's dilemma,
Least sail's through, nothing's tangible!
World needs results, we curse our boys!
At the fag end, there is nothing legible...

What is ruling the roost will keep ruling,
Ends never have a defined end!
What goes is vain are time and patience,
Others wait for an obedient transcend...

Among all we keep moving as guided,
By insights, people and prejudice...

ooo

106

The shape

These cars and houses, wealth and fun,
This me, my and myself, and the run...
To corner, to castle, to emancipate,
Shall keep bothering till we are done!

Time and age does never stop,
There is no harm, in thinking aloud,
Everything will pass and it's known,
They end up being, shameless or proud,

Gourmet of thoughts and the garments,
New peaks, bottlenecks and predicaments,
Of aplomb! And of differential beings,
Situations, their way, their ornaments...

There is no way but follow general,
It remains in shape, since it is readymade!

OOO

107

Doubt

The hare was smart, tortoise was dull,
In real life everything is void and null,
Things evolved, people accept disgrace!
Breaks are welcome, it's just a race...

The tortoise spoke and the birds flew,
His heart was lighter is saying adieu,
Loud mouths who cannot communicate,
Remain perturbed and live irate...

There was this crane which revenged,
On a fox who was already deranged...
Emotions changed, as a matter of motion,
Anger and pity lost in commotion!

Some adage, some stories voice out,
What remains in this heart is, doubt!

OOO

108

Another blink

To be in adventure and sweat,
To be in harmony and regret,
To be free once again,
Carelessness under sun and rain,

Being a child just with conscience,
Seeing, knowing, things anew...
The open smile without prejudice,
All accepting heart, while we grew,

The anger of not getting something,
Forgotten chagrin of a lost face,
The doing before even thinking,
The wish to win, just a race!

Simple things, yet so distant,
Easy life complicated forever...

OOO

109

The high of bad times

Better be quiet in doldrums,
Voice never communicates...
Chemistry, understanding, is nothing!
It's just the ego that elates,

One person becomes another,
All ruthless truth grow monstrous,
Who discovered the word "sane?"
When the whole world is preposterous?

Silence has its own abode,
Melancholy can survive death,
From one corner to another end,
Why love? Why not free breath?

Soliloquy has music, it's consummate,
It's always sound to be alone!

ooo

110

The beginning

I have left some and some worries left me,
Worries keep adding, time moves on...
People do forget restraints and realities,
Their own demeanour, where they were born,

Walking alive is not always control...
They watch us to change and die!
Their wishes coupled with accomplishments,
Their transacts, one cannot rely,

The edges rough and de-contoured,
Can't take away my spirit my smile...
I shall fight since fighting is life,
I will remain hungry and hence agile!

These worries can't take me over,
Beginning from zero is my nature!

ooo

111

Joy

If you struggle for nothing, you get nothing,
Few lived for a purpose, achieved mundane,
Topsy-turvy, this world has a speed...
It doesn't become, to use your heart or brain!

All awareness's are not knowledge,
You don't eat everything you see...
Unfortunate lot, and their futile thoughts,
Doldrums of graph, feeling to "disagree!"

The curves of life are too smooth,
We belong to the rough phase...
The rides are never soothing for us,
The tides are always disgrace!

One smile at the end of the day,
One moment of joy is all we wish!

OOO

112

Weaknesses

Only bright stars are visible, or I have stopped looking above!
Is there no space to see? Or I have learnt to bow down my head!
Time has changed, living has changed, silence has crept in...
Forgetting what I have earned, forever what I have read!

This cold and heat, keeps challenging people,
Weather is not the only thing that withers a mind,
Kith and kin and jobs and liking! The quest in finding...
Mockery of simple living, and farce of the mankind!

The evenings of age, bringing consciousness,
Alas all awareness's are not knowledge!
The broader senses, and bigger perspectives,
The weaker thought process can never gauge,

Nothing can admeasure the depth of thoughts,
Very few know the other soul!

OOO

113

Play

Either its greed or it's not agreed,
The numbers and timelines of life,
Living in contradictions alone...
Presence of absolute eternal strife!

One who smiles, keeps faking it,
Trumpets and tussles of power...
There is nothing sweet, only sweat,
When impulsive arguments shower!

We know we don't deserve unknown,
The joy of new, in blind folded prayers!
Things will change and rearrange,
Beautiful time spent as players,

I wish to play away from all,
No one to observe, neither me...

OOO

114

This being

If I don't deserve to say! Askance is my right,
If nothing is left for me, I am left with right,
Just trying to figure out, just trying to know,
What went wrong today, what's amiss tonight?

Bestowed my belief on very very few...
Yet there is betrayal, dismissal forever,
My survival to me is a matter of honour!
And what I cannot be, I shall be never...

They complete and complain of completion,
They think, and blink, their own predicaments,
Keep pushing from one threshold to another,
Soliloquy and chagrin, a well of sentiments!

I am alone and am happy for ever...
I am the way I am observed!

ooo

115

Contradictions

Hullabaloo has its own creativity,
The calm has its own rhapsody...
I wish and I want both of them!
Hence I am and shall be nobody,

Isn't it a matter to delve deeper?
Depth to our minds, is always grey!
Living our emotions in expectations,
Of how "they" feel and what "they" say...

This life belongs to people along...
Family, friends, co-workers and all!
The magic of occult, virtue of prayers,
Contradictions, in remaining small,

The dying wish for death is alive in many,
Sweat of sweetness is acknowledged rare!

OOO

116

The package

The pack of old friends discussing a package,
No one knew who left, and joined from where?
The beauty of a person and knick knacks,
A consummate! Challenging pens that fair...

The good, the bad, the bold and the clumsy,
Packages were alien, at one point of time,
People solemn? People benign and lost...
The tender age and the sweet rhyme...

Of differences that mellowed down to bonds,
Stronger than steel and taller than sky!
Brainless feelings, chagrin and joy...
That took them low, and then fluttered high,

In a pack of friends, it's more than a person,
Beyond name, shape, and virtues and vice...

OOO

117

The last leaf

It is some unwanted friends, who still care!
They still walk around, they still do fare...
It's only me and my selfish expectations,
I always look back with another flare...

When time grows old, keeps changing,
I run faster towards my death...
Challenges increase and expectations,
I remain gasping for another breath!

They still walk on along my sides,
They do abide a million jargons,
And takes the shape of my wish,
Lives on their own, for me like Nuns...

While I keep burning in my belief,
There is a story, "The last leaf"...

OOO

118

Own

Who is angry knows the truth and wrong,
Others just make sure they fake it...
A matter of befooling themselves!
With eyes wide open, they just take it,

To another wrong corner, of oblivion,
To another self and unknown region,
Not the Gods, neither the good,
They do boaster their own legion!

Yet we carry else's anger, chagrin and love,
Superfluous act of the know! unknown...
Isn't peace in truth and transparency?
What we shall reap, is what we have grown?

The sages asked to disown emotions,
It is so human just to follow the own!

ooo

119

Prudence

When all are young, it's a different life,
Then age catches up and expectations...
How parents survived against longings?
Why can't we live with our own creations!

Knowledge, prudence, is all shelved...
Not just they, we also know!
We might never accept the truth ever,
Yet truth is, we shall remain low,

Lower than expectations is mundane,
If mind is reeling, there is no Sunday,
Amongst wishes are only dreams,
Whom to argue with? What to say?

Those old days are in the wishful list,
There is nothing wrong in expectations!

OOO

120

Let them shape up

Thoughts keep running, everything is known,
Good bad ugly everything is known...
This conviction shall take me to hell,
I shall reap what I have sown...

This rigidity of not listening to others,
Stubborn, arrogance and confidence,
Another pit, self made, self derived,
Shall shape up my all confluence...

They shall remain as they wish to be,
In our dreams another dream wakes up!
While some call it idiosyncrasies,
It's a different plate, a different cup!

Feelings shall be nothing great...
The demise of one is demise of the being!

OOO

121

Disturbing

Life and people around shall keep pushing,
You chose your world and still continue...
Till the time we don't accept wrong choice,
There will be nothing great, nothing new!

Such is the common cause of all ailments,
All dissatisfaction, all chagrin and pain,
One leaves the game is one's choice...
The other keeps talking of some disdain,

Unfortunate few still have hope alive...
The fools the unread the absolute helpless,
With age their predicaments growing,
They remain afraid and beg for the restless!

Which is the natural being they know,
The disturbing truth they cannot efface...

ooo

122

Truth of a smile

I told tell tales, wanted to say more,
Time never respected free giggles,
Another life shall die another death,
Wish we stay agile, we stay singles...

The truth of life, the meaning of happiness,
Was and shall remain in freedom of birds...
We live and die and suffer as humans,
The way they repent, rotten in herds...

The mountains are my true friends,
They aspire, desire to outgrow...
In endeavours, in the cold beseeching,
They remain quite and low!

We shall meet again, we shall smile,
This parting is genesis to calm...

ooo

123

Man of the house

Trash for you is my treasure...
I am the man, who still belong,
To the same clan, the same vanity,
Still wish the childhood, carried along...

This age should grow with responsibilities,
Some become, others just fair...
We all are toiling to the same reason,
Against this face is only despair!

One day I saw someone without me,
The anguish the related turmoil...
Of one person being no more,
They still speak aloud, for this man's soil!

Chagrin can take you places? Belief!
The man of the house, has few dreams!

OOO

124

The winter of Delhi

While winter keeps roasting notorious plans,
And the fugitive mind has no slumber...
This city of concrete, smoke and thoughts,
Keeps counting lives, and all in number!

The ones who can buy, keep buying desire,
Of the simple, poor, ugly and old...
Wish to smile, in rotten blanket folds
The warmth of consummate, the eyes of bold!

Will there be no sun? And for never?
Wind shall keep playing cat and mouse?
This winter has smog of concerns and worry,
The wish to be someone else's house...

They walk down to burn earned currency,
Some keep their fingers crossed and wait.

OOO

125

Homogeneity

The homogeneity of seeds and animals,
Birds are the best with insects and worms,
Trees and humans are differently cooked,
Unhinged as always in different forms...

What if? Is just another glance to end...
The beauty of stagnancies, the lore of vision,
What shall never begin, be treated dead,
Why cant? Why not? Remains a treason!

They still come back, with a loud mouth!
Of god's, rituals and social blunder,
Unconsummated, irate and illegible...
They still can buy and flip a thunder!

Cows and dogs have been bred by men,
Trees and humans still have a choice..

OOO

126

The mortal

The most successful are also weird...
Family and instability, rock the world,
There are ways we try, make other's believe,
There are means that keeps us swirled!

The control of one, is disbelief of others,
All efforts, all jargons go to vain...
There are times when rhapsody remains,
There are moments we become insane!

If God is Generator, Operator and Destroyer,
Whatever shall be...shall only be!
Savings, ideas, future and past,
Shall never take a shape, never be me!

Nothing will change in our expectations,
No one can flip the mortal predicaments...

OOO

127

Wish to become

When I shall be helpless, I will remember,
The good old wine the healthy cucumber,
The dances of summer ecstasy...
My own friends and repeating December!

I don't wish to regret the past,
Hence enjoying today forever,
Broken tooth and a bad health,
Time can't compromise, can't cover...

Let dreams not be passed over,
There is enough in you and me!
This world, those cryptic hideouts,
So much to know, so much to see..

A sumptuous meal for empty stomach,
A wish to become, The You, The Me...

OOO

128

The deserved

A little more peace, little more money,
Is the genesis of trouble again...
What's wrong in being a cat or dog?
What's amiss in the whole bargain?

Prejudice and expectations alone!
The most disheartening disregard!
Of everything small and everything big,
No new moves, nothing left in card...

A little more mess, chewed with anger,
Some more trouble and dis-respect!
Many more probabilities, more confusion,
Every moment of changing perspect...

A little more love, a little more intellect,
Little more sleep, on the lap of death...

ooo

129

Far ends

When I am de-hinged, it's kind of accepted,
Where there are differences, something evolves,
Mine is generic, why are you bothered?
There are things, which never resolves...

You epitomise my far ends and all...
You bother me, disturb me forever,
These eyes, ears, limbs and balance,
Matter of age one must forget never!

Smiles turn into wrinkles,
Heart burns are never smoothened,
Aspirations remain afloat in dreams,
It's always the painful end...

Let them not rule the roost,
Let's live as we wish to...

OOO

130

The rare love

If they keep pretending, and if I know!
The dawn and dusk, shall be night and day,
The warmth of sun and the creamy snow,
Peace and slumber in blissful array...

One must forget to forgive for long,
It doesn't matter what remains agile,
The mind and heart in beautiful song,
The calm face and a child's smile...

A kid's love, shameless and clear,
Without physiognomy, without taste,
Continuity of waves in what appear...
Of a union where nothing is waste!

Laughter my soul, shall remain forever!
That's nature when we are one with it.

OOO

131

My world

I did make my own world, sometime back,
Still I am falling back on my past...
Things keep changing, rearranging!
Movements can't make commitments last,

This falling from positions, in-virtuous,
Beyond our control, before we can think,
Things keep changing, no one can believe!
Balances change within a blink...

The unknown saga of tell tales and all,
Bleak, to dark, to absolute invisibility,
World's get complicated, lost in pain,
Regaining motion, in sense and sensibility...

That world is lost, in dreamers repose...
Moving ahead defines success

OOO

132

The other side

What remains distant looks beautiful,
Hence the urge, hence the quest...
Realms of happiness I failed to board;
I am so sorry, yet I am the best!

In these thoughts, achievements, thrives!
It pulls, infatuates, allures and beckon,
The mind and soul and entire being,
Far off is the only stuff we reckon...

As dear, as near, the cause of happiness,
Giving a feeling, of being low,
To the mundane, meat, bone and flesh,
New reason for perpetual sorrow...

The journey and travel are like new love,
Grass will remain green, the other side...

OOO

133

Disown

Ah, this wish to disown you! before you do,
There is no feeling of love or adieu...
Then there is this heart, these thoughts,
I cannot be me, can never be you...

Brimming with a mind full of emotions,
Stupid love and caring and notions!
Why can't we refrain from movements?
What allures us to be in motions...

The new, the better and the craving for...
A change unknown, the genesis again!
How engrossed we all remain wishful,
Rudely deep and abominably insane!

This rule to prove, reign of faster...
Is so animal, yet so vanquished!

OOO

134

For the new born

When dreams come true, plants bear fruits,
At the top of the world, emotions elates...
Chagrin mellows down, caring begins,
In many folds, happiness translates!

Blessed are few, consummate are rare,
From the podium, vision is threadbare,
With little angels and lullabies around,
All that we wish, is to share and care...

This blissful feeling, this calm and joy,
For new born the universe is a toy,
You shall change the legacy to legend!
Let reign and victory, remain my Boy!

Your health, your peace, your equanimity,
Be as benign, as this moment of delight...

OOO

135

Rumble

Distance rumble, keeps rumbling,
Till impact there is no effort...
Neglect keeps the rumours growing,
When silence is broken, it's called noise,

Sweetness of calm and spice of change,
Is in ability to realign, intent to rearrange,
Swiftness of matter, stiffness of mind,
The savouring journey of self-trail...

Eyes and ears hummed by conviction,
Of only self and satisfied ego!
Even a rabbit or a bird can disrupt,
Peace so vulnerable so abrupt...

Shake off this day, dreaming of control,
There is no reign safe in slumber...

OOO

136

The connect

Your thoughts worry me endlessly,
It's not just bothering your peace,
There are many connected to us all,
Chains unhinge, with a pull of fleece...

Disruptive and self-designed problems,
For the sake of change, for new...
Makes things, people and ideas move,
Resurrect, disfigure and say adieu!

When one expects of accomplishments,
People along, run errands, to realign!
The penultimate and the desired echelons,
At the end nothing falls in line...

Yet one must move on, to know and see,
Cause unknown is always interesting...

OOO

137

The rock within

The rigidity of "I can", and fear of what next...
Suicidal combination, can upturn the living,
Where there is no recognition of what I get,
What only matters is what am I giving!

The wish for wholesomeness, the idea...
Perseverance for just accomplishments,
Whoever, whatever inspite of being in line,
If comes the way, deserves punishments,

As a child or adult, the existence to be,
Independent, admired, being worth it...
Is another space where the world stares!
The speed, the efforts, one must admit!

Devaluing things that are just natural,
Valuing self! Beyond expectations...

OOO

138

The new

The benevolence of "New", however trivial,
Brings happiness to a common person,
Space, people, tangible, or just a feeling!
All of us sometimes, are just anyone...

If it's momentary, paint it everyday!
No colours exists, beyond looking eyes,
"Change" and "new" are kith and kin,
This mind and heart should visualise...

Best and worst impacts are indifferent,
The root causes are new and old,
It's monotony or ecstasy that rules,
All our feelings, just unfold...

New is love and lust, old is grace...
This mind can't figure out justice!

OOO

139

Calm within

Rootless, uprooted or non-existent...
Disconnect is just another face!
Nature as always shall find its way,
Defying all antagonism, all race!

Mother and child shall remain within,
Distance, languages neither emotions,
Birth and death not mere difficulties,
Carry a string of similar notions...

Falling back on someone or something,
Rolling down to the basic DNA...
Is what happens over the long or short,
Rendezvous with obvious array!

Melting, settling, along that harmony,
Is where evolution takes a halt!

OOO

140

To forget

Tomorrow will always be new,
With your conviction or even without you,
New sun new people new places array,
Tonight with sore heart I say adieu...

To unhappiness, to unconsummated,
You tried today to the best of efforts,
Nothing changed, none realigned!
You are left to diagnose the cuts...

Pieces of pain and the mincemeat,
The common grind, and individuality,
The general mass shall keep moving,
Against the law of equanimity...

When animals can be happy with food!
Why do you look for another reason?

ooo

141

Hesitations

Hesitations took the better half and more,
Time never paused the journey or travel,
The longings, belongings were a part of it,
I was a morsel, still exist as a gravel...

This procrastination has taken a toll,
For the fortunate lot, it's fortune again,
Beyond an age, of self created realm,
Only thing that lives, is the bargain...

They talk of time and opportunities alone,
My wish for consummate, is still forlorn,
There is nothing that shall never be...
Mistakes of path and their glaring stone!

Being wrong, is albeit a thought!
Acting right is called wistfulness...

OOO

142

The slumber

The list gets smaller of good friends,
As life moves on, as living trends,
Mentality changes, priorities change,
Meandering the straights and bends...

Ultimate, penultimate everything is trash,
Once for all, one settles with likes!
Notions emotions are partners to it,
There had been love, there been spikes...

Of foolish living, trying for the best,
Of expecting to meet all expectations,
Of persuading, beseeching and praying,
Of cursing self for unknown aggressions!

The list moves shorter, contrary to age,
Slumber is once, when you are accepted

ooo

143

The sought peace

A faraway place, around unknown people,
Beautiful faces and amorous airs,
Along this mind there are memory lanes,
Across these thoughts what all not dares?

The journey of momentary to frozen,
The walk to know where one is fit?
Ages when peace will remain distributed,
Albeit the immense craving for it...

One must choose whatever the cost is,
Some things cannot ever be together,
The shorter calm is requirement of hour,
Longer quite is something we bother...

Trending with time and the wilderness,,
Is equanimity of another level!

OOO

144

Conviction

Convincing drains conviction at times,
Over askance slides obvious to oblivion,
Perseverance to revamp everything may,
Put you off! And put you on!

Not all journeys are always pleasant,
Something different makes them memory,
From a mundane travel to a happy bean,
Is that difference, which becomes glory...

Sticking one head, one brain to one thing,
Does not work always, fresh air deserves,
A lot more than just the change...
Is much more than what it serves!

In a way, new! Germinates and flows,
From one life to yet another...

OOO

145

Thoughts of a tide

For same feelings, expressions are other,
It's the situation not only people...
The facts of life, that shape and size,
Makes one bow and another steeple,

All of us feel, we are born to emotions,
Open to thoughts and our own notions,
Stagnancy is disliked for ever...
Still we all fear sudden motions!

If they do not move our expected way,
If it's really the body reaching to say...
An arrangement that does not suit us,
Or a part of truth, which can delay!

The dreamt, the expected path,
Of achieving one or disowning the other!

OOO

146

Bundle of thoughts

Again a bundle of thoughts tonight,
A free mind is under similar bondage,
Of wishing the wishful, praying, beseeching,
Looking for answers from old adage...

We all do things, with lot of things in mind,
Going wrong or right, is all about mankind,
Evolution or dis-integration takes years,
Yet truth is something we cannot find...

Entangled, embedded, in time and memory,
The emancipation remains under cover,
Freedom of the mind and the heart,
Is in forgetting thoughts, now and ever...

Bunch of people and munch of feelings,
Makes our lives much more difficult...

OOO

147

Jungle

The problem is never the one person,
It's the demeanour, the old habits,
It's a jungle, the nature, the mother,
Some are lions, some are rabbits...

Luck, fortune, intended behaviour,
That differentiated an animal, a man,
The advantageous, remained ahead,
Some early energy who planned and ran...

No point blaming comparison, amongst,
A bunch of minds without direction,
There is only unacceptance and dismay,
There is need for utter correction...

Once worldly! Family! Gets digested,
What moves on, is just conscience...

OOO

148

Neglect

Your neglect is another fuel,
Trust I don't accept this cool!
The journey is indifferent as usual,
You may be smart, I am not a fool,

It's all time, that rules the roost,
A pain of painting, the truth, the reel,
There is a value of everyone's time,
The recognition of the real...

Remains far off, yet the conscience,
The acknowledgement of the verity,
There is nothing but disbelief,
It's both of us who have anxiety...

Your disengagements are my folly,
Is like this life shall remain as it is....

OOO

149

To my mother

She still wants to talk...she is still curious,
With fallen eyes, she doesn't expect good,
All that she wants is good old days,
Caring now only for peace and food,

Not for herself, although kids have grown up,
Unheard and unattended, she keeps her health,
In her expectations words mince for others,
In her regular prayers she denies all wealth...

Alas old times of her sombre existence,
Unwanted yet the much known, agreed...
In disagreements when the life is spent!
For something else and unknown greed...

From this mind to the tip of my pen,
I am sorry mother, I disown myself...

ooo

150

Time and intent

You need a reason to leave the good,
Also for bad there are alibis...
When sense can't make sense further,
In unknown territories, time just flies!

Patching one thing, and creating one,
Are different in soul and in intent!
The fleeing away from a situation then,
Unattended shall remain in another bent!

Addressing the real issue for once,
Keeps fluid in our thought process,
This entire feeling of procrastination,
In guessing things would just guess...

Time rolls on, along with wrong,
Leave or take it, in the right spirit...

OOO

151

Half true

Between honest, dishonest, true and false,
These is no room for grey or other...
Between happy and sad, satisfied or not,
Very few one can accommodate another!

A little variance, comprises at times,
Create nothing but expectations!
One must stick to the heart and soul,
In every situation and all relations...

Ones that changed their normal course,
Are ones who probably don't know them?
And remain in a loop of contradictions,
Caught always in repeated mayhem!

A vicious circle engulfing everyone,
In comprising, being half true...

OOO

152

Undo

Sharing shared opinions, unworthy to the self!
Hearing and saying is unlike hear say,
We all commit, comment, convince on things!
Prudence and relationship, make their way!

Of time, situations, understanding estimates,
If burning is by nature, it shall only burn,
Alas we wait winds to change their course,
Albeit we all had our own turn...

In shaping a picture, we don't believe!
In spending time, in unconvinced notions,
In seeing things from another's eye's,
In agreement to falsify emotions...

Let's un-become, let's undress...
For the rest little, whatever is left!

OOO

153

Parasites

We are all parasites, living on the nature,
Nothing shall change barring our thought,
Why worried for other lookalikes and places,
What keeps the matter that matters not?

The reason for chagrin, for disappointment,
What keeps us reeling, tweaking our feeling?
Food, shelter, security, are all naturally provided,
When can we digest, the wholesome meaning?

What bothers is the time, the path and walk,
How well we shape and make others spend,
It's not a lonely journey, it's a caravan!
It always together, what begins or ends...

Asleep or awake one must endeavour,
In making oneself the part of nature...

OOO

154

Dear Daughter

Tomorrow is a big day for you my child,
I am with you now, and forever...
Somethings amiss in mundane routine,
These moments shall always give me shiver!

Why only a miracle or catastrophe?
Reminds me of being together?
This is another lacunae, complete failure,
Worried about this state like never!

Not just next, but all feelings of future,
The implacable me! Fails to accept...
Why only larger issues not small?
I am living, like I wish and percept,

Knowing what to ignore is knowledge,
Not knowing what to enjoy is death!

OOO

155

Names

I don't love you, just love your name!
Calling within myself makes me smile,
That name epitomised something's,
My love got allured meanwhile...

There's no truth but melancholy, and satire,
There is no one barring a little few!
Who comprehends the predicaments?
And acknowledge there is nothing new!

Some names are just expected to be nice,
While overall living remains falsified,
Albeit senses pull along with breathe...
You know you have been forever lied!

Those names are dreams, that do not become,
Their faces shall always remain in slumber...

OOO

156

A deep breath

Millions of humans and billion desires,
Morsels live on pieces they get...
Which God agreed? in what demography?
Still there are people, who love a pet!

Living small, unidentified, unknown,
Smaller the life, easier it is...
To remain away from competition,
To stay happy and to be at ease...

Ambitions competes with the small,
Greed compares with acknowledgments,
Morally weak shall keep abusing mankind,
Yet the meeker lot, seek accomplishments,

A hungry breath is just to show,
We can be a little different...

OOO

157

Crook and the crooked

The crook and the crooked were together one day,
They pondered and reached to some conclusions,
How can a poor labour laugh? Why old folks only pray?
They also agreed, all worries are nothing but illusions...

They pulled up someone, happy about nothing!
They asked each other for reason, but there was none...
If someone else is not disturbing one, it's insane!
There are no reasons to be merry, nothing to have fun!

Crook told the crooked his learnings from later,
Both were amazed by the way things keep shaping,
There was so much conviction in each other...
Own well-being, others misery, is best escaping,

They both agreed as always they did,
The crooked shall make only the crook happy...

OOO